UNLEASHING THE MIRACLES OF YOUR MIND

UNLEASHING
THE MIRACLES
OF YOUR MIND

HOW TO SET YOUR MIND FREE FROM
NEGATIVE THINKING AND GRAB HOLD OF
PERSONAL SUCCESS AND HAPPINESS.

SAL MAROTTA

Copyright © 2015 Sal Marotta

All rights reserved. This book or any portion thereof may not be reproduced or used in any manner whatsoever without the express written permission of the publisher except for the use of brief quotations in a book review.

Printed in the United States of America

First Printing, 2015

11 Jane Street
East Hanover, NJ 07936
www.salmarotta.com

ORDERING INFORMATION:

Quantity sales. Special discounts are available on quantity purchases by corporations, associations, and others. For details, contact the publisher at the address above.

Orders by U.S. trade bookstores and wholesalers.

Please contact Sal Marotta at
sal@smarotta.com or visit www.salmarotta.com.

CONTENTS

DOWNLOAD BONUS TRICKS AND
HELPFUL MP3S FREE!. 7

INTRODUCTION
THE JOURNEY AND THE ELUSIVE DESTINATION . . 9

CHAPTER 1
ENTER YOUR MIND 17
The Power of Thoughts 18

CHAPTER 2
THE SYSTEM. 27
Tier 1: Elimination 29
Squashing ANTs 36
Tier 2: Awareness 40
Meditation 40
The Benefits of Meditation 45
The Utility Belt of Tricks 48
Tier 3: Implantation 57
Hypnosis 69

CHAPTER 3
THE MIRACULOUS POWER UNLEASHED 73

ABOUT THE AUTHOR 79

ACKNOWLEDGMENTS 81

REFERENCES 82

DOWNLOAD BONUS TRICKS AND HELPFUL MP3S FREE!

READ THIS FIRST

We've found that certain practices can become infinitely more effective when used in coordination with this bonus content.

To thank you for downloading this book, I'd like to give you these helpful tricks, scripts, and MP3's 100% FREE!

www.unleashingthemiraclesofyourmind.com

INTRODUCTION

THE JOURNEY AND THE ELUSIVE DESTINATION

In today's world, we have access to so much helpful and inspiring information.

On a daily basis, we are bombarded with an endless stream of positivity posts on social media. We walk past the inspirational quotes hung on our walls. In our local bookstores, we have access to wealth of self-improvement literature. Why is it then, that despite all this, we still fail to establish habitual happiness in our lives?

Many of us, admittedly to varying degrees, have pursued many different paths in our quests to become the happiest and most powerful versions of ourselves. Sadly, a real grasp on an exciting, blissful, and productive life often eludes us.

Can you remember the last time you read or watched something so inspirational that you were convinced it would change your life? You probably can. And sadly, it probably had no real impact on your life at all. Have you ever been told that your mind possesses a miraculous power, yet you still feel you have not fully accessed it?

On a daily basis, we're exposed to countless forms of media aimed at convincing us that we can cultivate success and happiness. Despite this, we find ourselves navigating our lives with the lingering feeling that we haven't scratched the surface of our full potential.

The problem is that most of the information out there focuses on providing helpful systems that work *for* us, without taking the time to tackle the systems that are working *against* us. We will never change our lives by simply incorporating that one new belief or by watching a few inspirational YouTube videos. In order to end this internal struggle, we have to systematically destroy our doubts and the obstacles we perceive to be in our way and reengineer our minds to think productively and positively whenever possible.

THE JOURNEY AND THE ELUSIVE DESTINATION

We need to turn our minds into heat-seeking missiles that are locked in on happiness and success.

Whether we are seasoned in the pursuit of happiness, or new to the journey, we are all familiar with the feeling of being oscillated through ups and downs, while searching for new ways to improve ourselves.

While no single book will ever completely eliminate negativity from your life, there is a solution that will provide you with the opportunity to consistently create more happiness and success in many aspects of your life.

Unleashing the Miracles of Your Mind is a simple and effective system designed to help you destroy your doubts, purge your limiting mindsets, and fulfill your ambitions, while enriching your overall quality of life. This book will be beneficial to people seeking to make improvements to their levels of performance and happiness and to people who are repeatedly crippled by reoccurring doubts and negative thinking patterns.

As a lifelong student of the self-help industry, I have studied and experimented with dozens of traditional self-improvement practices. I have read countless books, practiced various forms of meditation, and undergone thousands of hypnosis sessions. In this how-to guide, I have comprised the best series of techniques, mindsets, and psychological hacks to help you manifest your wildest dreams and desires.

Students, teachers, athletes, and entrepreneurs have already increased their levels of performance and happiness by absorbing the insights and techniques offered by this system. With the tips and tricks in this book, you will have an essential checks and balancing system to unalterably tread your path towards happiness and abundance.

OVER THE YEARS, COUNTLESS PEOPLE HAVE BENEFITTED FROM USING THE TECHNIQUES IN THIS SYSTEM. HERE ARE SOME BRIEF TESTIMONIALS FROM THEM:

After applying the tips and tricks in this system, John, a student who spent four years struggling to earn a two-year degree at community college, put his life together and started to produce financial success in his life.

Tim, a medical school applicant, said, "the system helped me gain the necessary focus and reduced anxiety to exponentially increase my MCAT scores."

After thirty-four years of teaching, Anne, a middle-aged mother and middle school teacher, used this system to rediscover her passion for education and to cultivate a feeling of confidence in a workplace that featured an upswing of younger and increasingly innovative teachers.

Taylor reveals, "I never thought I could become more athletic by reading a book. But after applying this system for my own purposes I became a more confident and better basketball player than I ever could have imagined."

Max, a graduate from a major university with a degree in psychology, touches on how this system helps solve that dilemma. According to him, "Its greatest benefit is its ability to blend both the practices we are familiar with and new ideas into an easy-to-implement system that not only resonates with its reader but also produces unexpectedly powerful and consistent outcomes."

As Max reveals, this system converts some of the best self-improvement techniques available into an easy-to-consume guidebook that compensates for reoccurring negativity and offers you the opportunity to change your life. Whether you're a schoolteacher, a college graduate, or an athlete, this book will provide you with innovative insights on how to effectively tweak your thought patterns to ensure that you are capable of producing the results you desire.

In this how-to-guide you will:

1. Dig up and eradicate a series of mindsets that may unknowingly be holding you back from success
2. Learn various tricks and techniques to reduce the power of negative thought
3. Discover how to phrase positive suggestions in a way that will ensure outstanding results
4. Learn a collection of easy-to-practice routines that will allow you to habitually attract happiness and success
5. Unlock and utilize the miraculous power of your mind to develop new skills and attributes

There was once a time when I repeatedly thought that I needed the next piece of self-help material to nix my negative thought patterns and improve my quality of life. And then I began to wonder, if the answer was out there, wouldn't I have already found it? It was out there; it just wasn't presented in the right way.

I promise that this system, equipped with its three checks and balancing branches, will allow you to easily topple barriers that you thought were unconquerable and overcome doubts that you didn't even know you had. You will adopt a mindset that magnetically attracts success, and you will engineer you mind to produce positive and beneficial thoughts out of habit.

Don't be the person whose life is governed by highs and lows. Learn how to destroy your doubts and manifest your desires on command. Become equipped with the tools to find happiness in the here and now, and your life will be richer, happier, and more passionate than it ever was before.

As you will learn in this book, in order to have the life and confidence you desire, you must take deliberate action. You could pass up on this opportunity and keep searching for the answers, or start the end of your journey here and now. It's your choice. But if you're willing to learn and practice these techniques, you will unleash the potential to destroy your doubts and revitalize your life.

The passages you are about to read will reveal the system that is proven to release you from the restraints of doubts and limiting beliefs. Simply make a concentrated effort to keep reading and apply the suggestions provided.

Chapter by chapter, you will learn the three-tier system that will work in harmony to allow you to clear your life of persistent obstacles and allow you to finally achieve your desires.

Along the way you will encounter:

- ⭐ **TIPS**
- 🪄 **TRICKS**

I encourage you to write them down as you read, both to emphasize them and for convenient access later. As you will learn, writing down both your worries and desires can be an extraordinarily beneficial tactic for making change.

Take the first steps and begin to incorporate the techniques I'll be sharing with you in the following chapters – and watch as the life you've always dreamed of becomes reality.

CHAPTER 1

ENTER YOUR MIND

Unless you're my mom or dad, you're here because you want to change something. You may not be utterly depressed, hopeless, or desperate. You may not be plagued by constant and persistent negative thoughts. In fact, your life, by most standards, might be quite all right. However, like so many of us, you may be searching for a way to shake that lingering feeling of untapped potential. Whatever your case may be, the strongest piece of advice I can give you as we begin this journey is to remind yourself that you are alive, and you are already fantastic.

This is a powerful belief. And it is the beliefs that you buy into that determine your reality. Instead of adopting the belief that you need this book for happiness, remind yourself that you already have happiness in your life. Keep doing this, and I promise you that by the time you finish this book, you will already have made a substantial stride in the direction of happiness and success.

> ⭐ **YOU ARE ALIVE, AND YOU ARE ALREADY *AMAZING***

THE POWER OF THOUGHTS

The thoughts you have can do remarkable things. Have you ever had an important meeting early in the morning and set your alarm to wake you, only to find that you woke up minutes before the alarm even went off? By focusing on the idea of waking up at that time, you embedded a suggestion into your unconscious mind, and your unconscious mind worked to make it happen.

Have you ever performed a particular task extremely well in front of one group of people but performed miserably at the same task in front of different group? By holding different expectations and beliefs in front of different people, your unconscious worked to produce different outcomes.

Your unconscious mind is responsible for harboring an enormous collection of beliefs and expectations that both influence your daily outcomes and help create your reality. The reason that confidence is such a desirable attribute is because we realize that when we possess confidence, we possess thoughts that help us fulfill our desires.

*****

*As author and philosopher James Allen said,
"You are today where your thoughts have brought you;
you will be tomorrow where your thoughts take you."*

*****

When I was in elementary school I would consistently lose to my older cousin in a football video game. Honestly, it drove me crazy. So during my whole summer break I practiced the game intensely.

By the time school started up again, I was good enough to beat all my friends who had grown up playing the game. I had the technical skills and experience to absolutely embarrass my cousin over and over, yet when he paid another visit to my house, despite all my practice, he beat me. As I grew up, I continued to play the video game even when my cousin lost interest in it. To this day, despite my superior gaming skills, he still beats me every time.

Putting the childish example aside, my cousin beat me at the game (and continues to) not because he was a better player than me but because I had bought into the belief that I would lose to him. Even today, it doesn't matter that I know that my expectations will influence my reality, the images I give my unconscious mind direct my unconscious to issue me loss after loss.

Believe it or not, if you are familiar with competitive video games, you are already familiar with the power of your unconscious mind. When you first play a video game, it is largely a conscious task. You must memorize the controls, learn where the buttons are on the controller, practice your timing, and consciously focus on what is happening on the screen. However, as you progress, your unconscious mind takes over and you begin to do everything without thought. You don't have to think about what buttons to press and how to press them. You can devote your conscious attention to memories, daydreams, and conversations without losing a beat on the controller.

This happens because, through repetitive practice, your unconscious mind learns how to assume control and carry out certain tasks nearly autonomously. You may be aware of the many tasks your unconscious mind has learned to carry out on a daily basis. Riding a bike, driving a car, dialing a phone, and tapping your toe to music are all unconscious tasks. The unconscious learns these procedures through routine and repetition. Through the same repetition, it also learns to produce certain thought patterns, habits, and emotional responses.

By autonomously carrying out these procedures, your unconscious exhibits incredible power over your life. It can influence simple things such as the outcome of a video game challenge, or it could have a much more profound effect on your levels of happiness, productivity, and success.

By accessing and altering the beliefs of your unconscious mind, you can change anything, from your outlooks and mentalities to your skills and attributes. There are countless examples of people pulling themselves out of debt, overcoming insurmountable illness, and changing their outlooks on life merely by accessing and tweaking the contents of their unconscious minds.

When one of my college roommates, Nate, was in high school, if the weather was nice, he would often go fishing and boating in the lake outside his house. One afternoon, while driving around in his parent's boat, the boat made a sharp turn, accidentally catapulting Nate over board and into the water. Nate got sucked underneath the boat and his legs got caught in the propeller, severing arteries above his knee. He had to be lifted out of the lake by emergency helicopter, and when he arrived at the hospital the doctor was forced to perform an above knee amputation to save his life.

At the time, Nate's world had revolved around baseball. The amputation cost him his passion and changed his life forever. For months he was bedridden with the knowledge that he would never run or play baseball again. However, instead of wallowing in pity, Nate chose to affirm to himself every day, that if he could overcome death he could overcome anything, and even play baseball again. Every day he repeated to himself that his accident was blessing and that it would bring him untold gifts.

As Nate healed, he gained the ability to walk again with the help of a prosthetic limb. Against all odds, he took the mound again in baseball and pitched for his team. As a result, the American-based cable sports channel, ESPN, featured a segment documenting his recovery and his return to baseball. With his increased notoriety, he was offered the opportunity to throw out the opening pitch for a Tampa Bay Rays game. Nate continued to use the power of thought to turn his accident into a blessing.

He soon settled a lawsuit with the boating company and used the money to start a career in a prosthetic company. He now, despite his accident, has gained more experience with and exposure to the professional sporting industry than nearly all his high school teammates. He has started a career in a field he is passionate about, has become financially independent, and is helping people who suffer from amputations to reclaim their lives.

Nate didn't need all his arms and legs to fulfill his desires. All he needed was his unconscious mind. He adopted positive beliefs and established productive unconscious habits and used these tools to manifest his desires. If one manages to harness the power of their unconscious, he or she can bring all their desires into their life.

Unfortunately there are an equal number of examples of people who suffer through life because they unknowingly provide themselves with negative beliefs, supporting unconscious processes that dampen their levels of happiness and productivity.

A good friend of mine grew up as one of the most intellectually gifted children in our class. In elementary school, he was a member of every honors program, a straight A-student, and better versed in politics than I am now. However, somewhere along the line, in high school, he lost interest in academics. As his academic performance dwindled, our classmates' impressions of him changed.

While he was still as brilliant as I remembered him to be as a child, his classmates began to see him as remarkably unintelligent. They mocked him for his poor grades and academic failures. His teachers sent home progress reports, informing his family of his weaknesses and suggesting tutoring programs, reinforcing the affirmation that he was unintelligent. His younger sister outshone him by excelling in one of the most prestigious private high schools in the state, and ultimately going on to attend Johns Hopkins University too.

As the feedback he received from his parents, peers, and teachers reinforced the idea that he was unintelligent, I watched as my friend's brightness faded. He soon became intellectually tapered, less outspoken, and far less articulate. While I have no doubt in my mind that my friend's intellectual capacity was far greater than what he had represented, his beliefs about himself had handicapped him.

Take a moment to reflect on what the human mind can accomplish. As a species we have many physical limitations, but because of our capacity to think deeply we can recreate all the physical powers of the external world.

A hornet can kill forty honeybees in under a minute. The opossum can emit a protein that can counteract nearly any poison it becomes exposed to. A cheetah can run over sixty miles per hour. Elephants can lift more than 250 kilograms with their trunks. These are just a few examples of the physical gifts that us humans do not even come close to possessing. But what we have been gifted with is unlimited mental capacity and if we are not using the full capacity of our minds we can be likened to a cheetah that doesn't use its legs. The human brain has engineered vehicles that can move at nearly one hundred times as fast as a sprinting cheetah and has invented machines that are able to build towering skyscrapers that defy imagination. If a poisonous snake were to bite me, my physical body would likely be helpless, but because of the human mind we have created antidotes for countless poisons.

Do you really think you are not capable of starting a lucrative business or attracting your soul mate? The human mind, collectively and individually, can do whatever we will it to do.

Because of our ability to think deeply, our potential is boundless. The majority of this power stems from one division of your mind, a division few of us use to its full capacity: the unconscious. You may have heard the saying that we only use 10% of our brains. This is true—the other 90% percent they are often referring to is the unconscious. It is responsible for harboring an enormous amount of our beliefs and emotional triggers. While it is has a consistent influence on your everyday life, it is fundamentally different to the conscious mind.

Your conscious mind is your awareness. It perceives the sensations, functions, and surroundings within your immediate attention. Thoughts do not become conscious thoughts until they are brought into your awareness. The things that are merely within your perception are essentially the products of your conscious mind. The beauty of the conscious mind is that it is completely yours to control.

Think of your unconscious mind like an army. It is capable of traveling vast distances, conquering foreign lands, and demonstrating great feats of strength. Your conscious mind on the other hand, is like a General. It directs and provides orders for the army to follow. Each is reliant on the other. The General is useless without his army, and the army will never accomplish anything without directive from the General.

Believe it or not, we innately recognize the distinction between the subconscious and conscious mind. If you take a second to realize that you are reading this book because you hope to change an aspect of yourself, you will recognize the distinction between your conscious and unconscious mind. There is a degree of separation between your conscious perception of yourself, and the contents of your mind, which your conscious perceives. That is, your conscious mind *wants* change, and your unconscious mind will be *the subject* of change.

If we use our unconscious correctly and provide clear and focused directives to our unconscious minds, we will be able to use its power to manifest all our desires. Remember that your unconscious is an army, and while it is performs many actions autonomously, it always will abide by the directions of your conscious mind.

Has anyone ever asked you if you felt sick, or told you that you don't look so good, and then suddenly your body started to produce unpleasant symptoms? Perhaps your face lost color or you suddenly became nauseous. The mere mention of sickness can implant a suggestion in your unconscious mind that directs your body to experience symptoms of sickness. In the same way, human test subjects can be given a placebo pill in place of an adrenaline pill, and as result their heart rates will escalate, their blood pressure will rise, and they will experience the effects of an adrenaline rush without any direct chemical changes to their bodies.

Your unconscious mind is incredibly powerful, but it will always react to the directions it is given by your conscious mind. Now, I will ask you absorb another extremely powerful affirmation. Assure yourself that you have the ability to control the infinite power of your unconscious and you will be able to utilize it to its full capacity. If you incorporate this belief, all orders you give your unconscious will not fail.

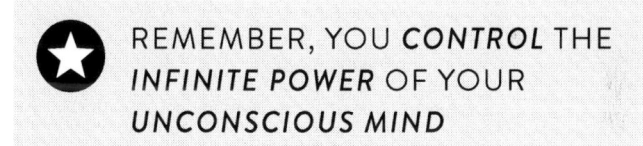

> ⭐ REMEMBER, YOU **CONTROL** THE *INFINITE POWER* OF YOUR *UNCONSCIOUS MIND*

With this statement you will assure yourself that the negative outputs and tendencies of your unconscious will never rule you and the negative inputs of the external world will always be within the control of your conscious filtration system. You can both choose what you buy into and what you allow your unconscious mind to absorb.

Incorporating this into your belief system is a great start, but beliefs themselves are only a piece of puzzle. Beliefs will only be fully effective when you learn to use them in a specific manner.

If providing ourselves with affirmations were all it took to become happy and successful, we would all be using these books as firewood to warm our million dollar yachts as we sail around the world. Unfortunately, few of us have yachts and even less of us have time to sail around the world. So what are we doing wrong? Are other things holding us back? Have we been given the wrong information? Is there a foolproof way to make sure my positive affirmations will change my life?

Yes, Yes, and Yes.

In the next few chapters you are going learn what exactly it will take to clear the path for mental success and to properly use your thoughts and beliefs to manifest your desires.

CHAPTER 2

THE SYSTEM

Over the next few chapters you are going to learn the three-tier system which will effectively teach you how to:

1 Conquer doubts and overcome negative thinking

2 Properly implant positive suggestions

3 Develop a mindset to manifest happiness and abundance

Each division of this system is structured to work independently as part of a checks and balancing system. Combined, they will allow you to abolish negative thinking patterns, and optimize the power of positive thought, always keeping you on track for success.

If self-improvement practices have failed for you before, this system will allow you to finally unleash their benefits. As you follow and incorporate the practices in each tier, you will eliminate the possibility of failure, and empower yourself with the ability to create whatever life you desire.

TIER 1
Elimination

Before you plant a garden, you must first pluck the weeds and prepare the soil. In the same manner, in order to make room for success in your life, you must first remove the trash and prepare your mind for it.

*In order to optimize the power of positive thoughts and suggestions, you must learn how to **free your mind from resistance**.*

Every mind has established its own habits and procedures that are often difficult to overcome. One of the driving forces behind me writing this book was to help those facing persistent doubts as they struggle to eliminate failure from their self-improvement practices.

While it may be easy to give yourself positive beliefs, it can be difficult to eradicate the negative beliefs as they fight back. Unfortunately, because of how easily the unconscious mind picks up habits, many of us have picked negative beliefs throughout our lives. These negative beliefs, convince us that it is not possible to make change and that our thoughts will always be conditioned to promote negativity.

I remember when I first read *Psycho-Cybernetics: A new way to get more living out of Life*, a revolutionary self-help book written by a pioneer in the field of self improvement, Dr. Maxwell Maltz. Maltz, a plastic surgeon, had observed how his patients' perceptions and beliefs about themselves had a tremendous influence over their reality. In his book, he used these discoveries to help people to enable their thoughts to work for them and to break free of self-limiting beliefs.

Fittingly, *Psycho-Cybernetics* was one the first books I had ever read on self-improvement, and for the first few weeks after I had finished it, it made me believe that I could accomplish anything. However, as time passed, and I dwelled on the power of the unconscious, I began to worry whenever I would think negatively. I feared that if a negative thought popped into my head that it was a disaster, and now that I allowed it to enter my mind, I would start producing negative outcomes in my life.

I wasn't aware of it, but subconsciously my own emotions had started to support this anxiety. Over time, I started to think that every negative thought was affecting my life. As I did, I began to incorporate this fear into my belief system. Because I believed that negative thoughts in my life were constantly influencing me, I started to habitually counter positive suggestions with more powerful negative thoughts. These counter suggestions often came in the form of "what if's."

If I affirmed that I could use my thoughts to create my reality, I was immediately met with a mental "what if," asking myself, "what if I can't control my thoughts?" or "what if I do, and they don't work?"

As I spoke with more people about their own positive thinking practices, I discovered that this is a common dilemma. Because of the negative systems we have already adopted, which endorse skepticism and label positive thinking as a new-age scam, we are encouraged to focus on the **possibility of failure instead of the expectation of success.**

Unfortunately, I too fell victim to this fear and this negative belief pattern spread. I began to believe that since I was so prone to countering every positive with a negative that I would start incorporating negative suggestions into other areas of my life. I feared that if I did, I would lose all my skills and attributes.

Sure enough, my belief made it so, and my doubts became more present. I lost confidence in many of my abilities, and what were once my strengths now became my weaknesses. By reading a book that was supposed to change my life for the better, I had actually handicapped myself. I decided that the solution would be to look for more self-improvement books hoping that the next one would help me right the ship. In doing so, I had adopted another damaging belief. I had bought into a self-help mindset.

Many people who read self-help books fall victim to this type of mindset, and it is one of the biggest reasons why the self-help industry consists of the same consumers buying book after book, without ever feeling fulfilled.

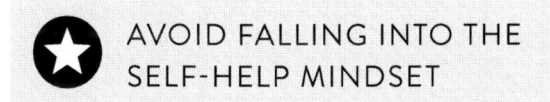

⭐ AVOID FALLING INTO THE SELF-HELP MINDSET

People who adopt the self-help mindset believe that they need the next self-help book to improve, and as a result, they cycle through stretches of confidence and stretches of depression. And if you're reading this book you may well be one of the millions of people who believe you're missing the next piece of information that will allow you to obtain true happiness. But if you want to obtain true happiness, you must accept that already have it, here in the present moment.

This is one of the most common handicaps people suffer from, and most aren't even aware of it. Believe it or not, you probably have many similar negative beliefs and mindsets holding you back right now. It will take the techniques in this chapter to truly dig them up and eradicate them.

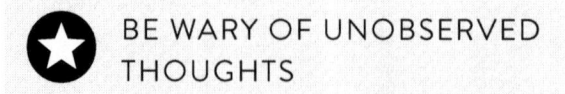

⭐ BE WARY OF UNOBSERVED THOUGHTS

While on the surface you might believe this book has already started to give you the tools to change your life, I encourage you to dig deeper and find the thoughts that are dwelling beneath the surface. Perhaps you have learned that positive thinking can greatly change your life, but underneath you are harboring the belief that eventually your optimism and motivation will fade, and you will once again have to search to rediscover your happiness. If you are harboring damaging dormant beliefs, they will slowly chip away at your energy and will limit the effects of positive thinking.

Whatever it is that you're doing, playing a sport, learning a new skill, aiming for a promotion at work — make sure that you're not harboring the wrong mindset. Believe that you're playing to win, instead of *not* to lose. Get open. Take the shot. Take risks. Risk aversion is a major limiting factor, and something we often unknowingly adopt in our fear of failure instead of desire for success.

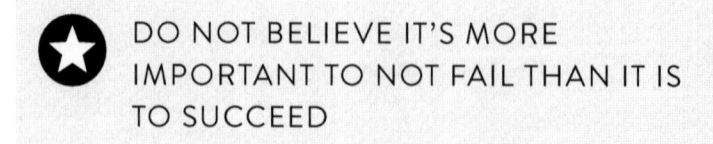

⭐ DO NOT BELIEVE IT'S MORE IMPORTANT TO NOT FAIL THAN IT IS TO SUCCEED

When you limit yourself out of fear of making a mistake, you unknowingly communicate to your unconscious that the only goal of your action is to avoid embarrassment or scrutiny, when instead the message should be a desire to achieve your goal. When you notice you are harboring this unobserved belief, push yourself out of your comfort zone and do what you are afraid to do. As long as the action won't bring harm to you or those around you, it will serve as a powerful tool to teach your mind to take risks. The more you push out of your comfort zone the more reference experiences you will have to convince yourself that you can accomplish things you fear you will fail at.

My friends and I used to practice a technique called *comfort zone challenges*, in order to become accustomed to pushing past our fears. These challenges would range from trivial tasks aimed at reducing our sensitivity to social judgment to extremely productive tasks that would help us feel more comfortable in taking risks while trying to achieve our goals. For instance, if we were trying to get someone to be less self-conscious when talking to other people, one of us would challenge him or her to walk backwards into a restaurant and with their back turned, ask the host for a table. By completing a task like this you expose your mind to your fear of social judgment, and you begin to learn how little it affects you if you do something embarrassing in public, which will allow you to become more comfortable when talking to people in the future.

Knowing that I enjoyed writing but was hesitant to make my work available for my whole school to read, a friend of mine once challenged me to submit a short story to my college's literary journal. I accepted the challenge and nothing bad came of it. In fact, I received more praise and compliments than I ever could have expected. Afterwards, felt a lot more validated in my skills. If I hadn't, I probably would have never gone on to publish my first book.

When you challenge yourself to carry out the tasks that you fear will result in failure, you learn how to overcome hesitation and limiting beliefs. So if you want to get the promotion at work, go talk to your boss and present your case, before someone else does. If you are a stay-at-home mom who wants to go back to school and get a degree, enroll in that online study course. Or if you think you have that next great American novel collecting dust in your computer hard drive, dig it up, edit it, and submit it to a publisher. You may not get the result you want, but if you don't take action, you will live your whole life wondering, 'what if?'

As you gain the reference experience of pushing past your hesitations, you will become more capable of doing so in the future and you will carry that energy into other areas of your life. The more chances you take, the more opportunity for success you will manifest.

> "The master has failed more times than the beginner has even tried."
> -STEPHEN MCCRANIE

Maybe after applying the techniques above you will begin to see great progress in your life. You may notice that your friends respect you more, that you are laughing more frequently, and that possibly your life's desires are beginning to unfold before you. However, you must remain conscious of the beliefs you are beginning to adopt. At first the effects of positive thinking might be rich and rewarding, however, like all things these effects will fade in and out. If your friends' respect for you isn't as apparent as it was before, and the laughs aren't as invigorating as they once were, do not allow yourself feel discouraged.

⭐ RECOGNIZE IMPERMANENCE

No positive feeling will remain as powerful as it was in the beginning, but if you begin to chase it when it starts to fade you will unknowingly enter a mindset of desperation. In order to more easily accept impermanence, you should readily practice the 🪄 **TRICKS** in the upcoming chapter. You will learn more about those later.

When you have learned to accept impermanence, you will feel more capable of allowing your confidence to remain robust no matter what your results. If you do so, you will avoid falling into a spiral of negativity, and you will develop the power to manifest your dreams whenever you desire. Recognize impermanence, and it will do wonders for eliminating negative thoughts. Remember, if you are happy, eventually it will pass. If you are sad, eventually it will pass too.

Unfortunately, too often, we latch on to happiness when it arrives, out fear that it will leave us, instead of embracing it. By doing so, we warp happiness into something else entirely. This is another belief you might not be aware of and that may be affecting your life. Try to live in the present moment and to accept emotions as they both arrive and leave. Do not anticipate happiness or sadness, or it will unknowingly affect your belief systems. Avoid these beliefs and you will no longer dwell on negative emotions, and suppress happiness.

However, there are more than just feelings of negativity. Our minds are littered with negative thoughts that show up in the forms of doubts and limiting beliefs. So besides recognizing impermanence, how do we get rid of negative thoughts? You have to squash them.

SQUASHING ANTS

Psychologists refer to reoccurring instances of debilitating thought as Automatic Negative Thoughts or (ANTs). ANTs can be habitual and damaging. You may immediately recognize some of the ANTs that emerge in your head on a daily basis. While they can't necessarily be completely eliminated, there are steps you can take to greatly reduce both their frequency and potency.

While negative thoughts can play such a large role in our lives, they are very often completely irrational. I can recall a vivid example of when an irrational thought popped up in my own life (and as you will learn, they often pop up in strange places).

I had once read an article on how to get larger servings of meat at *Chipotle*. To those unfamiliar with the restaurant, *Chipotle* serves its customers their food from behind a glass panel. The amount of food you receive depends on how much the employee randomly scoops up, unless you choose to pay extra. Following the instructions in the article, I approached the glass panel and looking the employee in the eyes, greeted him with a friendly hello and wide smile.

"I'll have a bowl please," I said in the cheery appreciative tone (which the article recommended). He didn't make eye contact. "Chicken please," I said. Again, no eye contact. He scooped a very light serving of chicken into my bowl. I moved down the line feeling disappointed in my ability to capture the employee's attention.

I just did everything the article told me, I thought. He must not like me for some reason. I must have seemed too eager. He definitely thought I was a people pleaser. I looked back to see the employee put a huge scoop of chicken into the bowl of the ninety pound fitness instructor in line behind me. I was shocked, and then immediately realized how critical of myself I was being.

It is crazy how frequently we judge and criticize ourselves for things that are out of our control. In the case of the *Chipotle* employee, it's likely that he wasn't aware of my efforts at all and and was merely lost in his own thoughts about his lunch break or unfed house cat. I had judged and condemned an aspect of my character based on the amount of chicken an employee had put in my burrito bowl. We comply with these negative thought patterns far too frequently.

Anyone who has taken an introductory course to social psychology may be familiar with the fundamental attribution error, where humans display the tendency to attribute excessive emphasis on internal characteristics to explain someone's behavior, rather than considering the external influences at play (*https://en.wikipedia.org/wiki/Fundamental_attribution_error*). We often engage with this pattern of thinking without justification.

Instead of assuming that the person who cut you off on the way to work did it deliberately because he was selfish and aggressive, assume rather that he did it unknowingly. The reality is that most of us (outside of New Jersey and New York City) are not aggressive drivers, but rather, we are preoccupied with our own thoughts, unaware we are inconveniencing anyone around us. It is not always the internal quality that is responsible: it is more likely the prevailing circumstances.

Unfortunately, we often blame internal characteristics when we are evaluating ourselves as well, as I did in line at *Chipotle*. Instead of placing the blame on our own attributes when we fail, it is just easy as for us to assume that a negative outcome is the result of some external and circumstantial influence. Choosing the latter option is much more beneficial to our moods and mindsets. Although, if another driver flips you off after you calmly let him cut off your minivan full of children, it would be appropriate to get angry.

⭐ ALWAYS TRY TO AVOID IMMEDIATELY PLACING BLAME ON AN INTERNAL QUALITY

Another major vulnerability we traditionally demonstrate is that of consistent comparison. As you may be aware, the media entices us to compare ourselves against unrealistic paradigms. For every made up, provocatively dressed swimsuit model on the cover of a magazine there are a million average-looking adults in society. Our focus, however, tends to reside on media archetypes. It is easy to dismiss the common notion that we can't all be as beautiful as celebrities, as athletic as NBA players, or as smart or well-versed as celebrity scientists. But how can we reduce the urge to compare ourselves to our more immediate peers?

Well for starters, the first step is to acknowledge when you are doing it. Our conscious awareness of the comparisons we make will allow us to look more deeply into the factors that play into our judgments. Are we really not as charming as our more popular co-worker? Or is it just that he or she grown more comfortable in our work environment than we have? Our tendency to believe the former instead of the latter manifests feelings of inferiority. Instead of allowing yourself to participate in these comparisons, measure yourself against yourself.

⭐ BE YOUR OWN STANDARD FOR SUCCESS

It may help to see other people's strengths as assets that have been acquired instead of gifts that they were given. By recognizing one's own strengths as accomplishments, you will begin to see more opportunities for your own advancements. There will always be people who are better looking or more intelligent than we are, but equally there will be as many who do not possess our unique attributes. In a way we all have our own gifts, but don't assume that because someone possesses something you don't, you cannot have it too. Remember that we all have unconscious minds and so we can all have whatever we desire as you will discover as you journey through this book.

By focusing on your own positive qualities, and defining other people's strengths as achievable, you will motivate yourself to develop in all aspects of your life. Consciously dismiss making comparisons to your peers, and you will develop internally. If you only seek to improve yourself you will remain protected against the disapproval of the external world. After all, you will only have yourself to impress.

Now for some people, these habits are easier said than done. But with this one tool, you can make these changes like clockwork. The key to developing and maintaining these habits is **awareness**.

By becoming aware and learning to monitor your thoughts you will prevent yourself from engaging with critical thought patterns and falling into a spiral of negativity. When you remain conscious of your thoughts, you will be able to rule them instead of allowing them to rule you. So how do you truly develop the ability to remain conscious of your thoughts?

TIER 2
Awareness

Numerous psychological studies have shown that by becoming aware of our internal dialogue, judgments, and biases we can reduce their power over us. When we recognize our thinking patterns we bring them in into conscious awareness. With increased awareness, we can monitor the effect they have over our unconscious mind. Through various studies on human psychology, we have learned how the conscious mind can be used to monitor and filter unconscious suggestions, or be completely bypassed to allow for suggestions to immediately penetrate the subconscious mind. If you learn to master your conscious mind, you will harness the infinite power of your unconscious for purely positive effects.

MEDITATION

Meditation has always fascinated me. When I was a child, I remember watching Star Wars cartoons on Sunday mornings and seeing glimpses of the Jedi characters practicing meditation. To me, it always seemed like a supernatural practice, something reserved for the characters from fantasy books and science fiction television programs. When I learned about real-life meditation, I was surprised by its practically and simplicity, but what shocked me most was its ability to actually have a supernatural impact on my life.

Meditation is one of the most effective tools to becoming conscious of your thoughts. As you practice meditating you will begin to develop a higher state of awareness. Among the most powerful discoveries you will make is that thoughts are merely thoughts, and if you so choose, they can have no effect on your mind. If you practice meditation you will learn that all thoughts, even the most persistent and damaging ones, can pass through your mind like clouds through the sky.

Meditation teaches you to release your grasp on all thoughts, so that in the future you have the ability to select the thoughts you want to follow and the ones you want to let go of. There are many different types of meditation, some with religious origins, and some completely secular. However, they can all be categorized as an offshoot or combination of these three elements: focused attention, presence of experience, and mindfulness.

You may experiment with the many different types of meditation to determine which method works best for you. There is an infinite wealth of resources both on the Internet and in religious texts and self-help books, to learn different meditation practices. However, in this text we will discuss mindfulness mediation, and the necessary pillars you will need to support a solid and successful mindfulness meditative practice.

The greatest benefit of practicing mindfulness meditation is its capacity to awaken us to what is happening around us moment by moment. And as we mentioned earlier, it will help you to recognize impermanence and live more frequently in the present moment. The goal of mindfulness is to simply be aware, and in turn, our awareness will teach us how to cope with our individual pains and distresses. It is crazy how often we allow ourselves to experience negativity without becoming consciously aware of its dominion over our lives.

There are multiple handy mobile applications, which provide schedules and audio tracks for different meditation practices. The *Headspace*[1] mobile application reminded me that we often recognize and draw attention to negative states of mind when they arise, but rarely pay attention to them when they subside. As we discussed earlier, we desperately hold on to happiness when it arises, out fear that it will eventually leave us, and we end up contorting it into worry and anxiety. As a result, we find ourselves submitting to negative energy and repelling positive energy.

While mindfulness meditation is a relatively simple procedure, there is so much room for expansion through study and practice. It might benefit you to follow a guided meditation program or to seek a meditation instructor to truly submerse yourself in the practice. Still, you can master the practice and reap its inexhaustible benefits by following these basic steps.

A thank you to author Karen Kissel Wegela Ph.D of *Psychology Today*, for reminding me of some of the following techniques in her article *How to Practice Mindfulness Meditation*.[2]

MINDFULNESS MEDITATION TECHNIQUE

POSTURE

To begin, you should assume a comfortable but upright position. You can choose to sit on the floor with your legs crossed or in a chair with your feet flat on the floor. Keep your back straight with your head up and, if necessary, place a pillow behind your lower back for support. You can place your hands on your knees or lay them comfortably in your lap. The most important factor is to maintain a posture that simulates awakened awareness. Your body and mind are intimately connected and a tired posture will lead to a tired mind.

Personally, I like to preface each meditation session with a sequence of five deep breaths. Breathe deeply through your nose, filling your belly with oxygen down through your diaphragm. Hold the breath for three seconds and then, release slowly through your nose. Try to expel the air from the bottom of your stomach to the top. Do this five times and you will already begin to feel your body entering a state of wholesome relaxation.

You can either choose to carry out the practice with your eyes open or closed. If you find yourself more inclined to daydream or feel tired when your eyes are closed, opt to keep them open. If you keep them open, focus your gaze softly, about six feet in front of you. Although falling asleep might be quite peaceful, it will only delay the benefits until your next successful meditation session.

At this point, begin to scan your body, observing for any particular sensations, pleasant or unpleasant. Perhaps your lower back is a little stiff, or your shoulders a little tight. Personally, I like to notice if my jaw is clenched, and if it is, I do my best to relax it. Just merely observe these sensations and allow your muscles to relax. Be conscious of the environment around you, the incoming sounds, smells, and sensations. If there is an air-conditioner blowing cool air along your neck or warm leather beneath your thighs, become aware of it.

BREATH

Once you have begun to become aware of your body and its sensations, concentrate on your breath. Watch as your breath moves in and out unconsciously, without any effort at all. Breathing is a natural habit of your unconscious mind, and it keeps us alive and fueled every day. As you are doing this, be sure not to alter your breath in any way, just observe as it enters and leaves your body. You may notice movement in your chest as you inhale and exhale, or maybe you notice it more pronounced at the back of your throat as the air enters your mouth as cool air and exits as warm air.

If you are having difficulty following the breath, count it as it enters and leaves. You can count repeatedly, one two, one two, counting one at the end of your inhale and two at the end of your exhale. If you choose to count, only do so after the breath has passed in or out, and do your best not to anticipate when it will enter or leave again.

Try to maintain the focus on your breath. When your attention is drawn away from it, which inevitably it will be, just gently bring it back to the breath. Remember that it is fine to lose the attention on your breath. The goal is not to merely focus your breath, but to observe what happens as you attempt to keep your attention on it. When you have observed that your attention has been drawn away, bring it back again.

AWARENESS

As you are concentrating on your breath you will notice thoughts and sensations emerge. Sometimes these thoughts can be incredibly magnetic, and they will attempt to draw you away from your meditation. Recognize that it is normal for these thoughts to arise, especially if you are new to the practice. It has most likely been a while since you were conscious enough to recognize that you are thinking, rather than being immediately swept up by that thought.

Remember, the goal of the meditative practice is simply to observe. You cannot succeed or fail at mindfulness meditation. The mere act of trying is beneficial in itself.

When thoughts emerge, watch them pass like cars in the street. Do not get caught up in the traffic. Just mentally wave at them as they go by. Sometimes when a thought arises, you can flag a note to yourself, "thinking" or "wandering" and refocus on your breath. If a strong sensation calls for your attention, observe it and gently watch as it fades.

Again, remember that you are not trying to stop your thoughts. Don't judge them or spin stories around them. If it helps, you can even thank yourself for having a thought, and then gently divert your attention back to awareness. Thoughts, just like your breath and sensations, are among the many experiences that you will observe during your practice.

THE BENEFITS OF MEDITATION

When you practice these techniques over time you will notice how you are more inclined to *observe* your thoughts than become *influenced* by them. As you repeat this practice, you will strengthen the neural pathways in your brain that support focus, emotional stability, and control.

An important aspect of finding success with mindfulness meditation is repetition. It is not necessarily how long you practice, but rather how often, that will determine your results. You are better off practicing five minutes a day for seven days a week, than 35 minutes a day once a week. Personally, I have found that setting aside 15 minutes a day for meditation is sufficient. You can choose to set a timer to remind yourself when the practice is finished, or you can just estimate. A little side note: if you do set a timer, keep it at a distance where it is out of sight and out of reach, so you are not tempted to check it as you are going through your practice.

At first, you may notice extreme frustration as you try to remain mindful. Many of us are conditioned to submit to incessant thought. However, when you become most frustrated is precisely when you most need the practice. I promise that over time the sessions will get easier and easier, and the frustration will fade away into the distance. If you are truly struggling with frustration, simply remember that frustration is just another sensation to observe. Do not judge it, or you will once again find yourself becoming lost in thought.

Once you establish a solid meditation practice, you will unleash a cascade of benefits. You will have equipped yourself with a powerful tool to filter the strength of your thoughts.

For me, the greatest benefit it provided me with was a reduced inclination from overthinking. I became more grounded, and my levels anxiety decreased tenfold. Instead of allowing the negative thought patterns to override positive thinking, I empowered myself to choose what thoughts I buy into.

When you overthink, you focus inward and confine yourself. The world becomes smaller, and the concerns you have seem to carry more weight. When you are free from overthinking, you become present to the world around you and other peoples' thoughts and feelings. If you free yourself from overthinking through meditation, you will notice how much creativity and compassion become apparent in your life.

Before I began meditating I was extremely neurotic, to the point where I would do an Internet research on every suspicious health symptom I experienced. After I started practicing, I was unbelievably more comfortable with my health and body. I even noticed that I manifested less negative symptoms, because I didn't over-analyze every abnormal bodily sensation that concerned me.

When I was in college and was experimenting with meditation, I walked into my college roommate's room and saw a statue of a giraffe in a Buddhist lotus position on his desk. "Do you meditate? "I asked him.

"No I never tried it," he told me. I had been experiencing the benefits of meditation for the last few years of my life, so I recommended the practice to him. After I demonstrated, he offered to give it a try for a week. He had such great results in that week that he continued to practice for the remainder of the semester (about two months).

By the end of the semester he went from being one of the most anxious and indecisive people I knew to one of the most calm and collected. Two months earlier, he could not send a text message to girl he was interested in without revising and rephrasing it for over an hour. Now, he dishes out text messages like a machine, and his relationship with women is stronger and more comfortable for both parties than it ever was before.

As you establish this practice in your life, you will find a stable resource for peace and happiness. By reducing chronic stress through meditation, you can make chemical changes to your body and improve your overall health. As you meditate, you will become more aware of harmony in your life and you will find more opportunities to become compassionate.

The beauty in music, friendship, and nature will become more apparent. The present moment will become richer and more vibrant. You will absorb more information around you, strengthening your intuition and receptivity. As a result, you will simultaneously become less judgmental, and you may even find yourself becoming more productive. But most importantly, meditation will allow you to become conditioned to use the infinite power of your thoughts without obstacles.

When you can monitor your thoughts, you can choose to use them or lose them. Meditation will clear your mind, relax your body, and increase your susceptibility to your own chosen suggestions. As your thoughts quiet, you will gain the ability to create images in your mind without the emergence of habitual counter-suggestions.

Fortunately, to succeed at overcoming the initial frustration of meditation, the weight is not all on our mind. The body is beautifully designed, and just as the mind can affect the body, so the body can affect the mind. Part of the design of this book, is to equip you with the tools to dampen your negative tendencies. In the next chapter we are going to equip you with some incredibly helpful tools, psychological hacks, and safeguards that will assist you with both your meditation practices and your overall peace of mind.

THE UTILITY BELT OF TRICKS

We discussed earlier the power of your unconscious mind to influence and shape your reality. However, the unconscious mind also plays another substantial role in your everyday life. While your conscious attention is focused on the tasks in front of you, your unconscious mind is constantly regulating your bodily functions. It keeps your heart beating, regulates your body temperature, and facilitates digestion. It is even regulating your breathing while you are reading this. Your conscious mind works constantly to keep your body functioning without conscious effort. While some of our bodily functions can be controlled with conscious effort, such as breathing and blinking, others are completely governed by your unconscious mind.

Two divisions of the autonomic nervous system control many of your unconscious bodily functions. Dr. Mark Hyman, author of *The Ultramind Solution: Fix your broken brain by healing your body first*,[3] reveals how the sympathetic nervous system, which regulates your blood pressure and heartbeat along with many other unconscious processes, is responsible for the activating stress response. While you can control the conditions that may trigger stress, you cannot control your sympathetic nervous system and its functions.

On the other hand, the parasympathetic nervous system, which governs "the relaxation response," is within some degree of our control. Our breathing, for instance, is an example of one of the unconscious procedures that we can control. By slowing it down and breathing deeply down through our diaphragm we can activate the parasympathetic nervous system and trigger a relaxation response. There are various activities you can do to stimulate the parasympathetic nervous system.

The beauty of being able to do so, specifically through your breath, is that it allows you to reduce the negative influences of stress. By activating the parasympathetic nervous system, you disengage the sympathetic nervous system, and thus you decrease your susceptibility to depression and anxiety, calm your mind, and balance your brain chemicals. You can induce a relaxed state of mind through various practices. When you do, you will realize that you have dampened the power of reoccurring negative thoughts.

The following **TRICKS** have helped many people reduce the persistence of negative thoughts. It is important, that while practicing each of them, you find a time and place where you are sure you will not be disturbed or distracted. This will be your moment to free yourself from the negativity of the outside world.

One of the most powerful practices you can use to calm your mind is deep breathing. It's remarkable how few of us use the power of our breath. We often go through our day unaware of the dwelling effect of stress. We remain unmindful of how shortly we breathe and what little we are doing to stimulate the relaxation centers of our brain. If you make an effort to observe your breath and participate in a deep breathing session once or twice a day you will do wonders for your sense of calm and tranquility.

DEEP BREATHING

In this deep breathing exercise you will learn to calm your mind and body so as to optimize your control over your thoughts and emotions.

Take a moment to sit straight up in your seat. Make your back perpendicular to the ground and pull your shoulders back. Now take a deep breath through your nose, breathing deeply down through your torso, expanding your stomach as you fill your lungs with air. Extend this inhalation process by inhaling slowly for four to five seconds or until your lungs are filled to capacity. When you have completed your inhalation, pause for one to three seconds holding the breath in your lungs. Now, release the breath slowly through your mouth, making sure to guide the air out from the bottom of your lungs to the top. The exhalation process can be as slow as you would like, but five to six seconds will usually suffice.

After you have exhaled completely you should notice a calming sensation flow through your body. Enjoy the pleasant and soothing sensation. Repeat this deep breathing pattern five times.

PROGRESSIVE RELAXATION

Remove your shoes and dress in comfortable, loose clothing to reduce muscle tension. You may choose to either lie down or sit in a comfortable chair. The most important factor is that your body remains supported throughout the practice. As you sit or lay down, take a deep breath, close your eyes, and relax all of your muscles.

When you are completely relaxed, it is time to start tensing your muscles. Focus on squeezing the muscles in one area of your body at a time. For instance, should you first focus on your face, tense all of the muscles in it, clenching your jaw, wrinkling your forehead, crunching your nose, etc, then systematically move down the areas of your body.

You should tense your muscles to the point where you feel rigidness and discomfort, but not to the point where you can hurt yourself. The goal is to target one muscle group at a time, without incorporating other muscles. For instance, while you are tensing muscles in your face you should not also accidentally tighten your neck.

After you have tensed a specific muscle group for about five or six seconds, it is time to relax the muscles. Immediately after tensing them you should rapidly release the tension. Make them loose and limp like a wet rag or a flimsy rubber band. After you have relaxed your muscles for five to six seconds, target the next muscle group, and repeat the process until you have tensed and relaxed your whole body.

In order to optimize the effect of the progressive relaxation process you should practice it in coordination with your breath. Tense your muscles upon inhale and relax them upon exhale. This will enhance the effect of each step and will result in a more satisfying relaxation response.

MENTAL TRANSPORTATION

This exercise could typically be classified as a visualization exercise. As we learned earlier, vivid imagination can communicate messages to the unconscious mind. The goal of this exercise is to use your imagination to create a vivid and sensory-rich environment, and to then mentally transport yourself into that environment.

In this practice, you should also begin with a deep breathing exercise. As you calm your mind with your breath, imagine yourself in a tranquil scene. This scene or place can be recreated from a peaceful memory or created completely using your imagination. Whatever you choose, be sure to saturate the scene with vivid imagery. If you are picturing yourself in a forest, imagine how the light shoots through the tops of the trees. Hear the leaves crunch beneath your feet as you walk. Feel the breeze whip through the branches of the forest. Reach out and touch the sap on the tree bark. Inhale the moist, earthy aroma from the dirt. Taste the salt on your upper lip as you sweat. Deeply immerse yourself in the senses of the forest.

It may help to interact with your environment, allowing yourself to discover new things and new sensations. Perhaps as you walk through the forest your legs get tired from scaling over rocks and across rivers. If you are walking along the shoreline of a beach, you may burn your feet on the hot sand and choose to cool them in the ocean water.

As you journey through this peaceful scene allow your body to relax. Reap the benefits of what a real visit to this sanctuary would do for you. Remember the goal of the exercise is to escape. Make sure to only imagine things that will help you relax. When the practice finishes, take these feelings of comfort and relaxation with you for the rest of your day.

✿ ✿ ✿

If you are having difficulty creating a vivid environment, there are various resources online that offer guided visualization exercises. My website *(www.unleashingthemiraclesofyourmind.com)* offers a series of free helpful visualization exercises with voice actors to guide you through the exercises. You can also find dozens of very capable guided relaxation videos on YouTube. Use these resources whenever you find the time.

○ ○ ○

If you want to optimize the power of your thoughts, you must manage your emotions, and these deliberate practices will allow you to do that.

Another powerful technique you can use to discharge negative energy is to create a worry journal.

WORRY JOURNAL

Set aside ten minutes every day to put all your worries into writing. By writing your worries down, you will give yourself a chance to observe them from an outside perspective. As you do, you may notice how trivial some of them are. Take notice of the worries that you don't need to carry with you and make deliberate plans to address the worries that absolutely require attention, in a timely manner.

What most people notice when they write in their worry journal, is that they are allowing worries that they can't do anything about to affect their emotional state and well-being. When you have taken note of these worries and recognized their triviality, tear out the worry page from journal and rip it up. By doing so you will communicate a powerful message to your unconscious mind. You will know that your worries have been addressed and you no longer need to let them plague you for the rest of your day. You will now feel free to fill the rest of your day with productivity and positive energy.

✿ ✿ ✿

These practices are specifically designed to help you relax and reduce the power of negative thoughts. However, there much more familiar practices that you can incorporate into your life to produce these same effects. Comforts, such as taking a hot bath, reading a book, listening to relaxing music, or exercising can have a profound effect on the mind. Carve out time for these luxuries in your life.

The beauty of these momentary escapes is that they absorb you in the moment and force you to become fully aware. In fact, any singular task that you can give your full attention to can be relaxing to both the mind and body. Make it a priority to eliminate distractions when you eat, watch a movie without checking your phone, and read or write without checking in on your e-mails. Modern technology has demanded us to divide our attention. As a result, we are more anxious and less in tune with our directives. If you want to free your self from procrastination, and reap the benefits of being in tune with one task, it may take a deliberate separation from technological distractions. When you become fully aware of and immersed in what you are doing you will become more relaxed and in control of your mind and body.

If you want to discover more tricks and psychological hacks to expedite your results, visit my website *(www.unleashingthemiraclesofyourmind.com)* to get some exclusive bonus content.

SMILE

Another technique you can use to elicit a positive response is a simple smile. Have you ever tried to smile when it wasn't natural? We've all taken pictures while grandpa's ripe underarm was wrapped around our shoulders, or with the weird neighbor's kid our moms forced us to be friends with. It can be incredibly uncomfortable, yet we peel back our lips and show our teeth like our mothers suggest.

The next time you are asked to smile, try to replicate a real smile. Smile as if you've just received that long-awaited promotion or were finally acknowledged by your crush. Show all your teeth. Squint your eyes. Pull the corners of your mouth up to your forehead, and hold it. You may notice that you will begin to feel positive emotions. By imitating a real smile we activate positive emotional centers in our brain. Our minds are conditioned to associate a smile with happiness. So when we smile, we are indicating to our brains that we must be happy.

In addition to these tricks above, you can eliminate negativity and balance your emotions through a healthy lifestyle. A whole food and nutrient-rich diet, proper hydration, and exercise will help make the chemical changes necessary to feel happy and motivated. I cannot emphasize enough the importance of taking care of your body, in order to take care of your mind. From personal experience I can vouch that staying hydrated, exercising, and eating healthily has optimized my mood and the power of my mind. Consult the wealth of well-documented research out there and resolve to pay as much attention to your physical as your mental health.

If you want to designate more research into the steps you can take to enhance your mind, by enhancing your body, I would recommend a book that I mentioned earlier, *The Ultramind Solution* by Mark Hyman.

❁ ❁ ❁

While the mere act of observation can reduce the power of negative thoughts, with a little conscious effort we can choose to replace negative thoughts with positive ones. Now that you have learned how to help eliminate the negative thought patterns from your life, it is time to reveal how to effectively incorporate positive thinking patterns. There are many positive thinking practices made available to us on daily basis, but unfortunately, many of them aren't very effective. Much of the advice made available revolves around positive thinking, but changing your infinitively powerful unconscious isn't that simple.

In order to allow your suggestions to have a lasting effect, they need to be given in a very specific way. In the next chapter, I am going to provide you with the simple and foolproof techniques of implanting suggestions, allowing you to avoid the pitfalls of most positivity practices and eliminate the risk of failure. I will reveal tried and tested techniques to using the power of thought to enrich your life, and you will learn the features that define a successful positive thinking process. By the end of the chapter you will have equipped yourself with some of the most important and elusive tools to manifest your desires.

TIER 3

Implantation

We discussed earlier how self-help gurus stress the importance of positive thinking. Positive thinking can have innumerable benefits. However, many people have been encouraged to take a misguided approach to positive thinking. They attempt to practice positive thinking and they ultimately fail, because they aren't effectively and clearly communicating their desires to their unconscious mind. As a result, they often give up on the practice before they can experience substantial results. Unfortunately, because of this, people conclude that positive thinking isn't nearly as effective or practical as advertised and very few people unleash its power.

I'm here to tell you that positive thinking, if practiced correctly, can be even more powerful than advertised. With the right components, positive thinking can give you the treasures that exist only in your wildest dreams.

This is one of the most powerful messages that people often miss:

It is not only *what* you think that influences your life but *how often* and *how intensely* you think it.

A thought here and there, will do nothing to change the habits of your mind. If it did, we would be reduced to a mindless mass every time we didn't know answer to a *Jeopardy* question or transformed into a modern day Don Juan every time a pretty girl smiled at us. A single thought is not that powerful, but repetitive and emotionally charged thoughts are infinitely so.

Most of us have tried positive thinking before, with little results. So where do we usually go wrong? Well, some of the most common errors revolve around two things, phrasing and diction.

⭐ BE CAREFUL HOW YOU PHRASE YOUR DESIRES…

When you tell your unconscious mind that you do not want to be poor, your unconscious mind conjures up the image of poverty. To illustrate this, I will ask you to participate in a simple experiment. Right now, try your utmost not to think of an orange caterpillar. No matter what, under any circumstances, do not think of an orange caterpillar. As we both know, you are, at this moment, thinking of an orange caterpillar. This simple experiment has been conducted over and over again in countless classrooms and textbooks. But why does it work? What message is this sentence communicating to your unconscious mind?

Embedded within the command, "Do not think of an orange caterpillar," is the command "think of an orange caterpillar." With this subliminal command, your mind is prompted to conjure the image of an orange caterpillar. See you did it again. (Hint: notice, "conjure the image of an orange caterpillar").

One of the most interesting things about your unconscious mind is that it struggles to process negative language. If you've ever seen a hypnotist, you may have noticed that they rarely ever offer commands using negative language, such as "not," "never," or "unable".

You too, should always phrase your suggestions in the positive. For example, instead of saying "I will no longer feel sorry for myself," say, "I am proud of and happy with myself." By phrasing things in the affirmative, you will project images of desire into your unconscious, instead of the images of disdain.

Affirming that you will no longer feel sorry for yourself, produces the image of you being sorry for yourself. Affirming you are proud of and happy with yourself, produces the image of you being proud and happy with yourself. As long as you phrase your affirmations with an image that inspires improvement, you will be well on your way to making your affirmations bring your desires into your life.

When you have begun to experience success and improvement in something, it is imperative that you stay conscious of these types of images. In order to avoid another pitfall that inadvertently gives your subconscious mind negative images, when you are measuring your improvements against memories of your inefficiencies, measure yourself in the positive instead of negative. The following example should help clarify what I mean.

Imagine you have just completed a course on public speaking. Prior to the course, you would sweat, stutter, and freeze up in front of large groups of people. Now you have finished the course, and you can speak confidently in front a crowd, project your voice throughout the entire audience, all while maintaining a strong and amicable posture. When you look back on your progress, focus on your new assets instead of your old faults.

It seems like common sense, but you would be surprised at how many people do the exact opposite. Many people focus on the image of their struggling self, and assure themselves that they will never fail like that again. Picture your assets now, and praise yourself for them, without looking into the past for comparison. If you continue to picture the positives without measuring yourself against your old faults, your strengths will continue to develop. However, if you look to the past to gage your improvements, the images of your past failures will dwell in your mind and encourage your faults to fight their way back to you.

My good friend was a competitive gymnast for many years. She recalls when she made a breakthrough in her beam routine by mastering and incorporating some high difficult maneuvers into her performance. With her new tricks, her scores at gymnastic meets had skyrocketed. She was consistently placing in the top three performers in every beam event in which she competed.

Her results were fantastic, but as she continued to focus on improving, she began looking to the past for comparison. She would attempt to gage her progress by looking back on a time before she mastered these new techniques, telling herself that she was so much better than she was previously. Unknowingly, while doing so, she was repeatedly providing her unconscious mind with images that showcased her previous failures. In an attempt to justify her improvement by looking backward, she started to regress. Soon she could not perform the high difficulty techniques to the same degree of expertise, and her scores began to drop.

Her coach asked her what she was thinking about as she tried to progress further, and she revealed she was attempting to convince herself that she could improve because of how much she had improved in the past. It took a complete overhaul of her thinking pattern to regain her expertise in the beam routine. Instead of using memories of the past to justify that she improved, she began to imagine, in vivid detail, performing the techniques to perfection in future meets. She restored her high level of performance and mental focus during the competitive season, and once again her scores skyrocketed.

> ⭐ **TO CONTINUE TO PROGRESS, DON'T THINK ABOUT HOW MUCH YOU'VE IMPROVED IN THE PAST... THINK ABOUT HOW MUCH YOU'RE GOING TO IMPROVE IN THE FUTURE**

You must remember that the unconscious communicates through images and emotions. If the images and emotions you project are not consistent with your desires you will never achieve them. For this reason, you have to be extremely conscious of how you phrase your positive thinking affirmations. Each variation in phrasing supplies your unconscious mind with different images.

If you phrase your affirmation in a way that projects an image of lack, it will be difficult for you fulfill your goals. A slight change in phrasing can completely alter the effect of your affirmation. For instance, instead of telling your unconscious "I *will* attract my soul mate," tell your unconscious "I *am* attracting my soul mate." While the former statement illustrates lack and suggests you will manifest your desire in the future, the latter suggests that you are already obtaining what you desire. Tell yourself you "will do" something and it will always be a day out of reach. Tell yourself you "are doing" something, and it will begin to manifest now.

> ⭐ **USE "I AM" INSTEAD OF "I *WILL*"**

Phrasing your affirmations with the word choice of "I *am*" will do wonders for wish fulfillment. It will provide your mind with an image that suggests you are achieving your desire in the present moment. However, images aren't the only language of your unconscious mind.

When you accompany your affirmations with emotion, you fortify their potency. Your unconscious is incredibly receptive to the language of emotion. I find it helps to load affirmations with power words. Power words are words that evoke powerful emotions. They may differ for everyone, but I have included a list of positive power words I often choose to include in my affirmations.

Grateful	Excited	Brilliant	Magnetic	Beaming	Attract
Effortless	Enthusiastic	Free	Naturally	Abundant	Prosperous
Vivid	Spry	Radiant	Young	Secure	Irresistible
Fast	Infinite	Peaceful	Reassuring	Profound	Rich

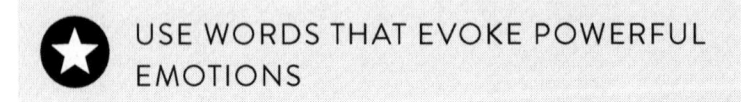

> ⭐ **USE WORDS THAT EVOKE POWERFUL EMOTIONS**

Vividly imagine your desire and feel the emotions you would feel after you have fulfilled that desire. Only then, will your desire begin to manifest.

If you want to sear a particular image into in your unconscious mind, envision it with all five senses. So if you want a new sports car, imagine how the car's exterior would reflect the beams of the sun. Picture its color and shape. Picture the clarity of the glass. Feel the texture of the leather as you grip the steering wheel. Smell the dry leather, burnished metal, and hand rubbed wood of the interior. Listen to the engine rumble as you start it up. Taste the flavor of your morning coffee as you drive your car to work. Make the image as vivid as possible. If you experience the details of your new car in your mind, you will convince your unconscious to accept it as reality. Because your unconscious communicates in the language of images and emotions, unlike your conscious mind, it does not have the capacity to analyze the objective reality of a specific scenario.

> ⭐ **THE UNCONSCIOUS MIND CANNOT DECIPHER THE DIFFERENCE BETWEEN REALITY AND VIVID IMAGINATION**

Our unconscious communicates and understands in the language of images and emotions and therefore, if an image is vivid enough or an emotion strong enough, it will speak to your unconscious mind. One of the most common examples of this occurs when you are watching a scary movie. Your conscious mind is aware that you are merely viewing a television screen. The screen showcases a series of pixels in motion. You are consciously aware that the pixels depict a cast of actors, mimicking real emotions, as they recite lines from a script.

As far as you are consciously concerned, the movie possesses no real or tangible elements and has no immediate impact on your life. Yet, as you inch up to the edge of your seat, grip your armrests, and watch as a shadowy figure scurries behind the unsuspecting blonde cheerleader, you experience real fear and anxiety. Your heart beats faster, your palms sweat, and you become infinitely more focused and alert.

It's remarkable enough that scary movies can affect you in the moment, but they can even cause lasting effects. They can make you fear staying home alone, wake you up in the middle of night with nightmares, and increase your levels of cortisol and anxiety for days. We would not be able to experience the thrills of a scary movie if it were not for our unconscious mind. Emotions, like fear, are a principle factor of your unconscious mind. By saturating your affirmations with emotion you will convince your mind of their reality. One of the most profound ways to do this is through gratitude.

It is not enough to know that you have made a change, you have to feel it. As mentioned earlier, I knew I could beat my cousin in the video game, but I didn't feel it. Gratitude is an essential part of the positive thinking practice, because once you feel grateful for an affirmation, you unleash its power. Gratitude will fortify your affirmations.

> ⭐ **IF YOU WANT TO MAKE RAPID CHANGE, ALWAYS USE IMAGINATION OVER WILLPOWER. WILLPOWER WILL EVENTUALLY RUN OUT, IMAGINATION WILL ALWAYS INSPIRE.**

For example, if you're on a diet, instead of willing yourself to resist eating unhealthy foods, choose to imagine the benefits of eating healthy foods.

Your mind is conditioned to believe gratitude follows accomplishment, and thus, by feeling genuine gratitude, you subliminally communicate to your unconscious mind that you have already achieved your desires. As your unconscious attempts to justify your gratitude, it will seek to fill in the missing link by manifesting your desire.

Another practical way of ensuring that suggestions become ingrained into your unconscious mind is through repetition. Most of the negative beliefs we harbor are the result of repetition. When you repeatedly supply your unconscious mind with a suggestion, it will inevitably begin to incorporate it into its belief system. Are you having relationship trouble? Examine your music. Do you repeatedly play songs about breakups on your radio? If you do, try changing the theme of your music. Listen to something that communicates a different message. Are you having financial trouble? Examine the articles and television programs you watch. Do they discuss the crippled economy? Read and watch material that highlights the opportunities for financial success and independence.

By repeatedly exposing yourself to negative inputs you condition your mind to believe you can't have whatever you desire. Now, make a conscious effort to counter those beliefs. Practice gratitude and assure yourself you can have whatever you desire.

EVERY NIGHT BEFORE YOU GO TO BED RUN THROUGH A DECK OF CARDS, AND FOR EVERY CARD, NAME SOMETHING YOU ARE GRATEFUL FOR.

Alternatively you can use a necklace with beads, a jar full of coins, a bucket of seashells, etc. As you name each thing you are grateful for, be sure to feel genuine gratitude. After practicing this trick for about two weeks, begin to use one or two cards to express thanks for things you have not achieved. Express genuine gratitude for your unfulfilled desires as well, and as a result, your mind will begin to believe that you already have them. Before you know it, these desires will begin to become features of your life.

You may also choose to write things you are grateful for down on paper and leave them in a gratitude journal. By putting the things you are grateful for on paper, you will reinforce the presence of gratitude in your life.

Below I have included a list of statements I have found have helped create change in my life:

I am so happy and grateful now that money and prosperity are flowing to me on a daily basis.	I am so appreciative that I live in a world of increasing wealth and abundance.	I am making whatever I want happen with the universal power of my thoughts.	I am calm, relaxed, and peaceful.
I am so grateful now that I consistently attract love and positivity into my life.	My ability to emotionally connect with and influence other people is growing every hour.	I am so happy that my mind attracts success in whatever I do.	Health, harmony, and peace of mind are beaming aspects of my world.

This system is tried and tested to produce results. I promise that by repeatedly asserting that you have obtained your desires, and emotionally embracing that you have fulfilled your goals, you will begin to notice immediate change in your life. Over extended periods of time, you can completely change your habits, rewrite your skills, and access unlimited resources.

> American author and transcendentalist Henry David Thoreau once said, "As a single footstep will not make a path on the earth, so a single thought will not make a pathway in the mind. To make a deep physical path, we walk again and again. To make a deep mental path, we must think over and over the kind of thoughts we wish to dominate our lives."

Allow thoughts of gratitude to dominate your life on a daily basis.

Various studies have shown that *it takes twenty-one days to a month to instill a habit.* You can completely change any aspect of yourself through repetition. It takes discipline and awareness, but if you make it a priority to incorporate these positive thinking practices daily over the next month, you will notice how by mere habit, your outlook on life will change. You must simply believe that you have this power within you, actively practice it in your everyday life, and your mind will provide you with the opportunities to fulfill your desires.

> ⭐ **REPEAT A POSITIVE AFFIRMATION DAILY, WITH GENUINE FOR 21-30 DAYS AND WATCH AS THE DESIRE MANIFESTS.**

American psychologist, Abraham Maslow, developed this model, which features the four stages of habit and skill formation:

FOUR STAGES OF LEARNING

STAGE 1: Unconscious Incompetence	Person is unaware of a particular skill and thus, is unaware he or she may possess some deficiency.
STAGE 2: Conscious Incompetence	Person is aware of a particular skill but still is in the process of developing the ability to perform the skill.
STAGE 3: Conscious Competence	Person can reliably perform the skill but must devote conscious concentration in order to do so effectively.
STAGE 4: Unconscious Competence	Person can now perform the skill without conscious focus, and the skill has become second nature.

https://en.wikipedia.org/wiki/Four_stages_of_competence

Right now you are most likely somewhere between stages two and three. You are aware of the effects positive thinking may have on your life, but you might be still developing the ability to effectively implement the practice on a consistent basis. By continuing with the practices above you will eventually transition into the fourth stage, and the mindsets and thinking patterns you have learned will begin to become unconscious habits. You will start to think positively without effort and as a result, your entire outlook on life will change. This model has been around for years, but very people take advantage of it. Try to progress through its stages and you will make improvements in many areas of your life. Use it to help guide you to obtain whatever new skill you desire.

HYPNOSIS

We spoke earlier about the power of unconscious suggestions and their ability to infiltrate your mind, shape your inner reality, and help manifest your dreams, goals, and desires. It is incredibly important, then, to arm yourself with all the tools to most effectively implant these unconscious messages.

To those unfamiliar with hypnosis, you might be either skeptical of its power or even frightened by it. Whatever your position, I encourage you to avoid associating hypnosis with an image of a strange mystic dangling a medallion in front of a helpless victim. To unleash the power of hypnosis, you won't have to sit down with a strangely dressed old man as he whispers, "you are getting sleepy," into your ear. You will simply have to relax and open your mind to change.

Hypnosis is actually far more natural than you may believe. In fact, we experience various forms of hypnosis throughout our daily lives. Essentially, when you enter a hypnotic state, you are entering a state of mind that is more susceptible to unconscious suggestions. No one who choses to dance like a chicken on stage is utterly opposed to dancing in front of people. The best part about hypnosis is that it allows you to influence your mind, while you remain in complete control. You have the freedom to enter and leave hypnosis on command and if you are consciously aware that you're being hypnotized, as all stage participants are, you can choose to either accept or refute whatever unconscious suggestions you are provided with.

Have you ever watched a television program while eating, and when you went to take another bite of your meal you realized it was already gone? Well, in this scenario, the dog did not eat your food, your conscious mind was absorbed by a hypnotic source (the television), and you completed an action without conscious awareness.

Have you ever yawned in a crowded room and noticed as other people began to yawn around you? Well, while their conscious minds were occupied by their own thoughts and external distractions, an unconscious suggestion was planted in their mind to yawn. Have you ever been riding in elevator, and as one crowd exited to a certain floor you followed them? These are all examples of everyday hypnotic experiences.

Media advertisements, magazines articles, political campaigns, even other people, are both intentionally and unintentionally, providing you with hypnotic content, bypassing your conscious filter system and implanting suggestions into your unconscious mind. Unfortunately, many of the external suggestions we absorb are designed to get us to buy something, or to behave in a certain way that guarantees someone else's profit. I am going to reveal how you can hypnosis for your own profit.

Hypnosis is a powerful restorative tool that you can use to deliberately influence your mind. You can use it to both alleviate problems and to fulfill your desires.

Above, we discussed repetition, gratitude, and positive thinking as viable solutions to change your unconscious beliefs and tendencies. Here, you will learn how to use self-hypnosis as another tool to change your thoughts, behaviors, and reality.

PRACTICE SELF-HYPNOSIS

When you enter a state of deep relaxation, your mind becomes more susceptible to unconscious suggestions. As we noted earlier, when relaxed, your mind can focus more clearly and you become more capable of making changes to your belief systems. So, to strengthen the effects of a hypnotic session, you should first relax your mind and body. In order to do so, put on comfortable clothing, sit in a chair with your back supported, and implement one of the relaxation practices described in the previous chapter (again, the deep breathing practice is ideal). After you have relaxed, you can begin the hypnotic process.

As you relax you will notice your eyes begin to get heavy. Allow them to close. With your eyes closed, affirm to yourself you are about to enter a hypnotic state. Repeat out loud to yourself, with conviction, "As I get more relaxed, I am starting to access my unconscious mind."

After you have repeated this phrase a few times, and your body is beginning to feel limp and relaxed, imagine yourself standing at the top of a staircase. As you look down at the staircase, notice there are ten steps. Continue to breathe deeply. With each deep breath you take, take a step down the staircase. With each step you take, you will be walking further into your unconscious mind.

Repeat these phrases as you descend the staircase.

- **10** You are becoming more relaxed
- **9** Your muscles are loose, limp, and relaxed
- **8** You are going deeper into your unconscious mind
- **7** You are infinitely more relaxed now

You can continue the pattern of these suggestions until you have completely descended the staircase. Feel free to tweak the above statements in whatever way makes you feel most comfortable and relaxed. The goal is to emphasize relaxation and unconscious suggestibility with each step, until you reach zero.

When you have reached the bottom of the staircase, you are free to begin providing your mind with unconscious suggestions to inspire change. You can choose to affirm whatever you wish. You may use some of the positive affirmations above, or you may create your own affirmations. Just remember to phrase them in the positive. If you follow the phrasing suggestions discussed earlier, you will reap more profound results from your hypnotic practice.

When you have planted the desired suggestions, begin to ascend the staircase, with each step becoming more alert and aware of your environment. By the time you have scaled the staircase, you will be ready to return to your normal everyday activities. Thank yourself for taking the time to implant your desires, and affirm that you are awake, refreshed, and ready to take on the rest of the day.

※ ※ ※

If you enjoyed this hypnotic session, I encourage you to expand your practice by looking for new and more elaborate hypnotic inductions online. This session was designed to merely serve as a rudimentary, but effective, model of self-hypnosis. With a quick search on any Internet search engine you can find websites and articles that offer excellent tricks, tips, and hypnotic scripts available for your self-hypnosis practice. My website also offers some of these bonus features.

CHAPTER 3

THE MIRACULOUS POWER UNLEASHED

As I was writing this book, I continued to practice many of the techniques above. Every day, I charged myself with positive energy and motivation. I repeatedly affirmed that the infinite power of my unconscious mind would help me to publish a book that will help people change their lives. However, about halfway through my writing, I began to manifest doubts.

Despite all my work, I encountered what seemed to be a major obstacle. A fatal flaw had jeopardized my book's chance of getting published. This being my first book for a major publishing platform, I was unsure how to tackle the problem, and I began to lose motivation. On the morning I was about to give up, I received an email with a link to an informational video by a best-selling author, on writing your first book.

In the beginning of the video, the author touched on my problem. At the end, she encouraged people to reach out to her if they had any questions. Immediately after I followed her advice, I sent her an email thanking her for her brilliant talk, and informing her of my obstacle. Little did I know, she would respond. An hour later, she sent me an email with the exact answer I was looking for. My problem was solved, my motivation was restored, and I continued writing. By mere circumstance, I was put in contact with a best-selling author, who was capable and willing to help me destroy my obstacles with one quick email.

The following day, I lost my last set of car keys. I paid a visit to a local locksmith to get a new set. They had the keys I was looking for but they had to program them to work in my car before I could use them. For the next two days, I waited as they tried to program my keys, but a manufacturer error had complicated the process. The mechanics told me that because of the specific year and model of my car they might not be able to make the keys compatible. They informed me, that in order to get a working set of keys, I might have to take my car to a dealership and make a serious investment. For a twenty-two year old with no job, this is a monumental problem.

Despite the disappointing news, I continued to affirm that the mechanics would figure out a way to fix the problem. The next day, I got a call from the mechanic. He told me that for some strange reason he got the idea to program the keys backwards, following the exact opposite procedure his manual instructed him to. Even he admitted the idea was bizarre, but he tried it anyway, and it worked. He handed me two brand new keys saving me a ton of time and money.

Many of us have gone through moments in our lives when it seemed as if everybody and everything were working against us. However, by altering the patterns of your unconscious mind you can flip the script. You can engineer the universe to work for you. I have been thoroughly practicing these techniques for three years now, and the results are undeniable.

Against all odds I have accomplished tasks that I once only dreamed of— even when the naysayers sought to plant doubts about my abilities in my mind. I have dealt with my self-limiting beliefs and negative unconscious patterns. I now live my life in a state perpetual excitement because I have opened my mind to receiving the gifts life has to offer here in the present moment.

Over last few years, I have noticed that people seeking to improve themselves often yearn to recapture the confidence and joyful anticipation they experienced as a child. They wish to restore outlooks and demeanors younger versions of themselves once possessed. However, they fail to recognize that these younger versions of themselves weren't constantly measuring their levels of happiness against the feelings they had in their past.

Instead of looking to *past* to gage your happiness in the *present* moment, recognize that here and now you can access the miracles of your mind. Using these techniques you can free yourself of negative thought patterns and self-criticism, and establish unconscious beliefs that will help to manifest your desires.

Remember, you are human, and that is enough to make your wildest dreams come true.

A professor once said to me after my graduation that no one can know what the future might hold for you. I have never disagreed more. You will learn from experience that it is the act of knowing that determines what your future holds. Know and believe that you will obtain your wildest dreams and you will have them.

If I can do it, you can do it.

Here you have many of the most useful tools to both create your desires and eliminate your doubts. You are armed with a system that can change your life. The system is simple and universally applicable, but it can be tailored to become as complex and specific as you may like. Only by employing the tips and tricks above, will you truly experience how the world can work for you. With the right practice, the universe will begin to help you manifest your desires.

If you incorporate the power of positive thought into your everyday life, you will begin to see miraculous results. After a while, it will seem like the entire world is working to alleviate your problems and turn your dreams into reality.

Incorporate gratitude into your life, not only for the things you have, but for the things your family and your loved ones have as well. Express thanks, and you will notice you have abundance. Observe and let go of your thoughts and negative emotions as they attempt to fight back. Practice taking risks. Gain the confidence, through your affirmations, to challenge yourself. As you do so, you will gain the reference experiences to deeply believe that you can create whatever you desire.

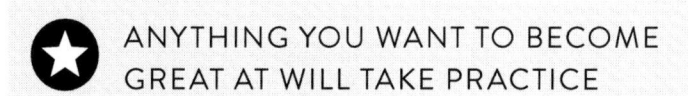

⭐ ANYTHING YOU WANT TO BECOME GREAT AT WILL TAKE PRACTICE

If you want to learn to dance, you have to practice dancing. If you want to learn to drive, you have to practice driving. If you want to change your life, you have to practice changing your life.

You will need to do more than just read this book once. Read it again and again. Incorporate these new beliefs and practices into your everyday schedule. Discuss these principles with your friends. Make each other accountable for consistently following these guidelines. When you fall off track, refer to your notes. Only through repetition, will you achieve your desires. But if two things in this world are worth practicing, they are happiness and success.

There will be times when you lose motivation or feel like giving up, but remember, these are the times that it imperative that you push forward. Keep practicing. Keep affirming. Imagine resistance as a rubber band. Its pull backward will always be strongest when you are just about to break the band. Don't snap backward, break the cord holding you back and find your freedom.

Now, the system is yours, and it's up to you to do with it what you choose.

Good Luck, and may this world become your playground.

I NEED YOUR HELP!

Thank you for downloading my book!

I love when people give me feedback. It's so helpful to know what really resonates with my readers.

If you want to let me know what I'm doing right or help me make the next version better...

Please leave a helpful REVIEW on Amazon.

Thanks!! You Rock!

ABOUT THE AUTHOR

SAL MAROTTA

Salmarotta.com

Since an early age, Sal Marotta has been a student of the power of the mind. Beginning his journey by studying and practicing magic tricks, Sal progressed into the field of Mentalism and hypnosis. He quickly learned the various ways in which the mind can influence reality.

When he started his college career, he was a psychology major, but knowing his current path of obtaining a BA and then attending medical school held a long road ahead of him, he chose an alternative path, one that would provide him with the opportunity to make an immediate impact.

After a year and a half of majoring in psychology, Sal switched his major and obtained his Bachelors of the Arts in English from Rollins College. Upon graduation he received Marian Folsom Jr. Award for the genial quality of scholarship — leavened by warmth, wit, and modesty. He is a published author of multiple works for the Rollins College *Brushing Art and Literary Journal*.

Today, he has taken the passion he had for one subject and the skills he learned in another, and has used them to provide people with opportunity to create the lives they have always dreamed of, the lives they know they are entitled to. Wanting to capture the tools that only select few of successful people have had the opportunity to get their hands on, Sal made it his priority to get his hands all over them.

He is now privileged with the opportunity to share his discoveries with people all over the world, helping people to maintain positive and productive lives, to build better relationships, and to find confidence in themselves.

For more information about booking Sal Marotta as your speaker for your next event, contact him at *sal@salmarotta.com*.

ACKNOWLEDGMENTS

A thank you to Chandler Bolt and Self Publishing School, for whether they know it or not, really helped me to get this book out there.

A thank you to all the self-help teachers, and professional speakers, who have paved the way in the field of self-improvement. Were it not for the discoveries and contributions of Maxwell Maltz, Napoleon Hill, Dale Carnegie, Anthony Robbins, Wayne Dyer, Eckhart Tolle, and many others, my work would have no foundation to stand on.

A thank you to my professors Jana Mathews, Emily Russell, Jill Jones, and Matthew Forsythe for provided me with the tools to effectively communicate my ideas.

A thank you to all those I forced through endless revisions of this book.

And finally a thank you to my parents who have always supported me and my endeavors, and whose character and positive spirit inspire me on a daily basis.

REFERENCES

1. *Headspace.* Computer software. *Apple App Store.* Vers. 2.3. N.p., 27 July 2015. Web.

2. Wegela, Karen K., Ph.D. "How to Practice Mindfulness Meditation." *Psychology Today.* The Courage to Be Present, 19 Jan. 2010. Web. 11 Aug. 2015.

3. Hyman, Mark. *The UltraMind Solution: Fix Your Broken Brain by Healing Your Body First: The Simple Way to Defeat Depression, Overcome Anxiety and Sharpen Your Mind.* New York: Scribner, 2008. Print.

*Names have been changed to protect privacy.

Printed in Great Britain
by Amazon